DUBAI

THE CITY AT A GLANCE

Vision Tower
The 260m angled-glass office to
in 2011, is the most interesting
cluster, although that's not say
Al A'amal Street

Business Bay
An extension of the creek, the waterway was a
dead end until the 3.2km Dubai Canal opened
in late 2016, linking it to the sea at Jumeirah.

Jumeirah Bay Island
Another man-made island, this is a mini version
of The Palm, shaped like a seahorse. It hosts
the Bulgari hotel and some very tony villas.

Old Town
If you don't have much that is historic, why
not build it instead? The mixed-use development
here is a melding of pan-Arabian influences.

Burj Khalifa
The world's highest tower is one of the most
beautiful pieces of architecture in the city.
See p073

The Address Downtown
Now restored and revamped, after a fire that
engulfed it was broadcast on live TV just before
the official 2016 New Year's Eve fireworks.
See p016

The Dubai Mall
In the world's largest mall (for now), you can
ice skate, scuba dive and try a flight simulator.
Financial Center Road, T 362 7500

The Index
Foster + Partners' 326m eco-friendly office and
residential giant is set in a 200m-long pool and
accessed through a four-storey open-air atrium.
See p076

INTRODUCTION

THE CHANGING FACE OF THE URBAN SCENE

Beneath its Middle Eastern veneer, Dubai is really Asian. Arabic is the national language and Islam is the official religion, but while you will hear a 'salaam alaikum' or two, Arabic is notable mainly for its absence. As indeed are the Emiratis, who account for about 10 per cent of the population, South Asians for more than half.

A Gulf state with limited oil of its own, Dubai is an economic powerhouse. Poised between Iran, the still unstable Iraq and the hard-line Islamic republic of Saudi Arabia, the city is relaxed and fairly tolerant. It also has global clout, although its population is only two and a half million. Since the 2008 crisis, expansion plans have been revised. But still the projections are for another 900,000 residents and 20 million tourists by 2020. Impossible? Maybe. But that's a word rarely heard in a place that modesty never visited. And now that the speed of development has picked up again, spurred on by the forthcoming Expo, it has resumed its vaulting ambitions.

Perhaps it's the squeaky-clean urban environment. Perhaps it's the good life. Whatever the draw, people keep on coming. *Stepford Wives* perfect in parts, Dubai is a giant resort in a construction site. Love it or loathe it, it is a phenomenon that tempers its bad habits (it's environmentally unsustainable, and fractured along class and racial lines) with an unshakeable conviction that everything can and should be changed. Dubai is all about upward mobility, and in a region currently in turmoil, that alone makes it a marvel.

ESSENTIAL INFO
FACTS, FIGURES AND USEFUL ADDRESSES

TOURIST OFFICE
T 600 555 559
www.visitdubai.com

TRANSPORT
Airport transfer to Downtown
The metro runs from Terminals 1 and 3
to Deira and along Sheikh Zayed Road
www.rta.ae
Car hire
Avis
T 220 3800
Public transport
www.rta.ae
Taxis
Dubai Taxi
T 208 0808
Careem
www.careem.com
There are also cab ranks outside shopping
malls and the larger hotels

EMERGENCY SERVICES
Ambulance/Police
T 999
Fire
T 997
24-hour pharmacy
Life Pharmacy
Al Wasl Road/Al Safa Street
T 224 7650

EMBASSIES/CONSULATES
British Embassy
Al Seef Road
T 309 4444
www.gov.uk/government/world/
united-arab-emirates
US Consulate-General
Al Seef Road
T 309 4000
dubai.usconsulate.gov

POSTAL SERVICES
Post office
Al Wasl Road near Jumeirah Civil Defence
T 600 599 999
Shipping
UPS
T 339 1939
www.ups.com

BOOKS
**The Architecture of the United Arab
Emirates** by Salma Samar Damluji
(Garnet Publishing)
Dubai Architecture & Design
edited by Sabina Marreiros (Daab)

WEBSITES
Art
www.alserkalavenue.ae
Newspaper
www.thenational.ae

EVENTS
Art Dubai
www.artdubai.ae
Design Days
www.designdaysdubai.ae
Downtown Design
www.downtowndesign.com

COST OF LIVING
**Taxi from Dubai International Airport
to Sheikh Zayed Road**
AED60
Cappuccino
AED20
Packet of cigarettes
AED10
Daily newspaper
AED3
Bottle of champagne (duty-free only)
AED200

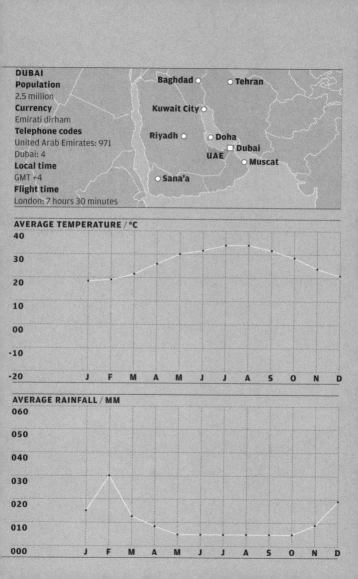

DUBAI
Population
2.5 million
Currency
Emirati dirham
Telephone codes
United Arab Emirates: 971
Dubai: 4
Local time
GMT +4
Flight time
London: 7 hours 30 minutes

Baghdad ○   ○ Tehran

Kuwait City ○

Riyadh ○   ○ Doha
                 □ Dubai
          UAE
                 ○ Muscat

● Sana'a

AVERAGE TEMPERATURE / °C

```
40
30
20
10
00
-10
-20
     J  F  M  A  M  J  J  A  S  O  N  D
```

AVERAGE RAINFALL / MM

```
060
050
040
030
020
010
000
     J  F  M  A  M  J  J  A  S  O  N  D
```

NEIGHBOURHOODS

THE AREAS YOU NEED TO KNOW AND WHY

To help you navigate the city, we've chosen the most interesting districts (see below and the map inside the back cover) and colour-coded our featured venues, according to their location; those venues that are outside these areas are not coloured.

MARINA

Spanning the southern flank of the city, this is the apotheosis of 'New Dubai'. It encompasses the very vertical Marina, the swish Emirates Hills (all showy villas and irrigated lawns) and the visible-from-space Palm. For the well-heeled expat families that live here and party-loving locals it attracts, nothing else matters.

AL QOUZ

A dusty, industrial neighbourhood where much of the city's manufacturing is still done, Al Qouz is the location of a blooming creative scene. Many of its warehouses have been converted into galleries, and a smattering of cafés (see p045). Alserkal Avenue (see p032) is now a major art hub.

DIFC

The original business district, the strip of glass towers along Sheikh Zayed Road has merged into the newer, shinier DIFC, the spotless banking centre. Its refined restaurants (see p046) and upmarket galleries (see p071) pull in the expense-account types, as well as stylish expats.

DEIRA

Cramped, chaotic and crumbling, Deira could not be less like modern Dubai. This warren of laneways will finally give you a proper sense of being in the Gulf. Survey the souks, tour the city's first school (see p033), take in the Clock Tower (see p012) and ride the water taxis that ply the Creek.

DOWNTOWN/D3

In a place with an excess of urban 'hearts', Downtown has established itself as the core. The draws are the astonishing Burj Khalifa (see p073), the opera (see p078) and the many eateries of faux-historical Old Town, like La Serre (see p056). D3 is gradually maturing into a Design District as envisaged by the government.

BUR DUBAI

The child of the 1960s building boom looks a little rough around the edges, but it is home to excellent Indian joints and a hefty chunk of architectural heritage. Big draws are the old houses of Bastakiya, Al Fahidi Fort, and the well-restored but no longer lived in sheikhs' residences in Shindagha.

JUMEIRAH

An almost-empty stretch as recently as the 1970s, Dubai's premier seaside suburb has a relaxed air, with a mix of villas, cafés and boutique malls. Chill on the pristine public beaches, hang out at The Espresso Lab (see p041) and browse the upscale shops, such as IF (Umm Al Sheif Road, T 394 7260).

CREEK

Winding towards the wildlife sanctuary of Ras Al Khor, the Creek turns from bustling waterway to leisure space. On its northern side are the Dubai Creek Golf & Yacht Club (see p077) and Festival City, an enclave of shops, bars and restaurants. Opposite here is a whole sorry mess of construction.

LANDMARKS
THE SHAPE OF THE CITY SKYLINE

In Dubai's pancake-flat landscape, its countless towers provide the only punctuation. But while their number continues to increase (with the merest pause following the 2008 financial crash), very few stand out from the clutter. The elegant spike of Burj Khalifa (see p073) and the sail-shaped Burj Al Arab (see p015) are the icons, but have been turned into clichés by their inescapable presence on T-shirts, postcards, carrier bags, incense burners and paperweights. This lack of inspiration is disappointing in a city that has based its reputation on superlatives (the tallest this, the most luxurious that) and it's ironic that a few pre-1980s structures that somehow escaped the wrecking ball are among its most accomplished (see p011).

Given that the recent interventions are noticeable rather than noteworthy – 2017 saw the addition of the Dubai Frame (Zabeel Park), two 150m-high towers joined by a 93m sky bridge, bizarrely designed to actually look like a window frame – perhaps it is best to consider the landmark question on a macro, and not a micro, level. From its beginnings as a speck on the map, a former pearl-trading town where airlines would touch down only because they had to refuel, Dubai has been transformed into a sprawling, rapidly metastasising city that, shades of Ozymandias aside, is convinced it is not simply a global hub but *the* global hub. Forget individual buildings, Dubai's most impressive landmark may just be itself.
For full addresses, see Resources.

Cayan Tower

Until it was christened after its ego-trip developer in 2013, the Cayan Tower was known as Infinity – an appropriate name for its helical form, if not such a fortunate metaphor for the repeated delays caused by engineering problems due to its site on a man-made promontory. Designed by SOM and anchoring the north end of the Marina mega-development at 306m, it is the most imaginative building here. Each of its 75 floor plates is rotated slightly from the one below, resulting in a 90-degree twist from bottom to top. Apparently, this helps combat wind load and solar gain, but the benefit for the observer is the way it captures and reflects the light at different times of day, adding tremendous aesthetic appeal and giving it a presence far stronger than that of its taller neighbours.
Dubai Marina Walk, www.cayan.net

Sheikh Rashid Tower

Ask a taxi driver for Sheikh Rashid Tower and you'll most likely get a blank look. The cream-coloured icon is so firmly ingrained in local folklore that even recently arrived cabbies call it the 'Trade Centre Tower'. The 149m building was a pet project of Sheikh Rashid bin Saeed, who commissioned Brit architect John Harris, creator of the city's first masterplan in the 1960s, to devise a skyscraper to serve as a blueprint for the future. To universal surprise, he sited it far from the centre and, at the 1979 unveiling by Queen Elizabeth II, it was surrounded by sand. Today, it is the gateway to the wall of glass that lines Sheikh Zayed Road. Its distinctive design (1970s modernism with references to regional iconography in the windows' arched shape and deep frames) is depicted on the 100-dirham banknote. *Trade Centre Roundabout*

Deira Clock Tower

Although Dubai's centre of gravity shifted to the other side of the creek and points further south many decades ago, the Clock Tower remains embedded in the affections of long-term residents. Finished in 1964, when Dubai had only one paved road, it marks the Deira side of Al Maktoum Bridge, the first structure to span the waterway, which had been completed the previous year. The clock was a gift to ruler Sheikh Rashid bin Saeed Al Maktoum from his son-in-law, Sheikh Ahmed of Qatar. Held aloft on slender, curved brackets, which evoke classical Islamic architecture, at roughly three storeys high, it used to soar above the desert but has been dwarfed by surrounding development. The supports had to be rebuilt in 1989, as the unwashed beach sand used to make the concrete had leached salt into the steel reinforcements. The clock's four faces endured until 2008, when they were replaced with Omega dials.
Clock Tower Roundabout

Emirates Towers

These equilateral glass-and-steel triangles, designed by NORR and completed in 1999, rise 305m and 350m. The smaller houses the Jumeirah Emirates Towers hotel, and the other, offices, including that of the PM and key government departments, and was the city's highest finished structure for a decade. The pair have been compared to bottle openers and pencil sharpeners, and are linked by The Boulevard, once the most exclusive mall in the Emirate. These days several luxury brands maintain a presence and its restaurants continue to be a draw (see p032). A swathe of the 17 hectares of peacock-populated landscaping that's part of the complex has been taken over by the Museum of the Future, an arresting, silver-clad, hollowed-out ellipse designed by architect Shaun Killa, slated for late 2017. *Sheikh Zayed Road, T 330 0000*

Burj Al Arab

Critics say that it resembles a giant Teflon beetle sitting on its haunches, yet there is something undeniably magnificent about this hotel on first sight. Viewed from afar, it appears to catch the breeze, like the dhow sail that inspired WS Atkins' design. It's only when you get up close you truly appreciate its scale – at 321m it is one of the tallest hotels in the world. Once inside, your impression may not be as charitable.

The palette in the 180m-high atrium is eye-popping, and the floor-to-ceiling aquarium engulfing the Al Mahara restaurant is pure fairground. That you need a reservation in one of its restaurants or cafés to even be allowed across the bridge is hubristic, but no doubt the guests paying thousands of dollars a night to stay in its gaudy suites prefer not to be invaded by rubberneckers.
Jumeirah Beach Road, T 301 7777

HOTELS

WHERE TO STAY AND WHICH ROOMS TO BOOK

It is unfortunate that Dubai's most famous hotel is also its most garish. Thankfully, the self-styled 'seven star' Burj Al Arab (see p015), aka the hotel that taste forgot, is not representative. Hotels feature heavily in Dubai's expansion and all its new 'cities' include a couple. Some of the most hyped are in a cluster comprising a W (see p022), a Westin and a St Regis in Al Habtoor City. Meanwhile, The Address Downtown is set to make a comeback in 2017 on the same spot as it was famously gutted by fire on New Year's Eve 2015, and has already launched a splashy sister, The Address Boulevard (Mohammed bin Rashid Boulevard, T 423 8888) nearby.

Amid the glitz, there are at last a few more choices that combine style and intimacy. The XVA (see p024) has still not been matched by anything as small and quirky, but Vida Downtown (see p028) scores for cosmopolitan chic, as does the Bulgari, which brings the brand's high gloss (courtesy of Antonio Citterio Patricia Viel and Partners) to an island off Jumeirah Beach. Dubai doesn't really do budget, although the Rove group launched in 2016 as a moderately priced option; Rove Downtown (312 Al Sa'ada Street, T 561 9000) is perhaps its most conveniently located property. Thanks to all the openings – even Mayfair stalwart Dukes (T 455 1111) has been recast as a resort on The Palm – it's no longer a nightmare to find a room in peak season (seemingly any time except summer).

For full addresses and room rates, see Resources.

Park Hyatt

Nestled between the two halves of Dubai Creek Golf & Yacht Club (see p077), the Hyatt's whitewashed Moorish exterior, with its glistening blue cupolas, *zellige* tiles and lush tropical greenery, hints at the glamour within. The public spaces, such as the Palm and Fountain gardens, and pool (above), are all understated and elegant, and the light-filled guest rooms are pitch perfect; choose a Park Executive Suite with a patio overlooking the Creek. Open-plan bathrooms mean that couples should either know one another intimately or be ready to gain that knowledge. The sleek Amara Spa (T 602 1660) and wood-panelled Traiteur (T 602 1814), offering French bistro fare and a superb wine cellar, help make the Hyatt a one-stop haven. *Dubai Creek Golf & Yacht Club, T 602 1234, www.dubai.park.hyatt.com*

Armani Hotel
Located in the Burj Khalifa (see p073), the Armani Hotel has the designer's stamp all over it, from the furniture to the spa products. Guests are treated like royalty, and the minimal interiors offer relief from the gold and gilt elsewhere in the city. Standard rooms, such as the Armani Classic (pictured), are small; the larger suites boast fantastic views. *Burj Khalifa, T 888 3888*

Four Seasons DIFC

With its discreet entrance, modest scale and low-key vibe, the Four Seasons DIFC could hardly be more different from its gargantuan sister property located on the beachfront in Jumeirah, which opened a year earlier in 2015. Like most city-centre Four Seasons around the world, it feels grown-up and quietly confident. And while that translates into somewhat unexciting decor, the polished woods and neutral palette give it the feel of a sleek New York club, as in the Deluxe One-Bedroom Suite (opposite). Other rooms are quite compact but well-designed, and the bathrooms are super-slick. There's an American diner-style restaurant, a rooftop bar that draws a crowd in the evenings, and the cosy Penrose Bar has become something of a hideaway for locals. The top-floor glass-walled pool (above) is a standout feature.

Building 9, Gate Village, T 506 0000, www.fourseasons.com

W

The much-hyped W opened in 2016 in a tower beside Dubai Canal. Nobody could accuse it of being low-key; even by W's standards, this is up to 11. The interiors, by Singapore's Silverfox Studio, were designed 'to evoke the speed of Dubai', not least the traffic roaring by on the 12-lane Sheikh Zayed Road. It translates into multi-coloured stripes throughout the public spaces, the effect amplified by mirrored surfaces. Bedrooms (Marvelous Room, pictured) are more subdued, and done out in a palette of white and greys, although the 'floating' furniture, curved walls and cut-out cornices can be quite disorienting. It's not especially tasteful, but if flamboyant is your thing, it's rather fun. And isn't that what the W is about? *Al Habtoor City, T 436 6666, www.wdubaialhabtoorcity.com*

XVA Art Hotel

Housed in a renovated coral-stone-and-adobe home sheltered within the quiet, maze-like alleyways of the ancient traders' quarter of Bastakiya, XVA is unique. Not only does the charming property give its guests the chance to experience an upscale version of life in a Dubai that disappeared 75 years ago, but the tasteful way the 14 rooms have been individually decorated, one with darkwood furniture, curtained bedsteads and mother-of-pearl-inlaid furnishings by Karim Rashid and Lebanese designer Nada Debs, is a delight (although mind your head on the low doors). There's a gallery, a boutique and a café. The breezy roof terrace is a refreshing spot to unwind on steamy nights and the courtyard (above) is the place to kick back in winter.
Near Al Fahidi roundabout, behind Arabian Tea House, T 353 5383, www.xvahotel.com

Grosvenor House

From the drink and the chilled towel that greet you on arrival in the marble lobby to the fruit plate set out in your room, the Grosvenor is a class act. Standing alone when it was built a decade ago, it is now surrounded by the Marina's high-density towers, although it has lost none of the cosmopolitan glamour that made it a hit from the start. The blue-neon exterior lighting belies the graceful interior, which has a cool Asia-meets-Middle East feel that is carried through to the rooms. Beds big enough for a party, views over The Palm, Bulgari toiletries and restaurant Indego (see p060) make for a seductive package. If you happen to tire of the in-house pools (above), guests have access to the Royal Méridien's private beach across the road. *Al Sufouh Road, Dubai Marina, T 399 8888, www.grosvenorhouse-dubai.com*

La Ville
A residential and retail quarter of low-rise buildings across several blocks, City Walk is the paradigm of a humanised approach to development that has emerged since 2014. In the evenings, the pedestrianised street that weaves through the shopping area is the scene of Dubai's version of the passeggiata. In the midst of it all, La Ville opened in 2016. Designed by Woods Bagot, it's a welcome addition to the city's limited stock of small, stylish hotels. The decor is all clean lines and pale, neutral tones; it might not be wildly original, but the simplicity is refreshing. In the bedrooms, wood floors and furnishings add warmth and there are large-scale illustrations of the 'hood. The Chival restaurant (T 403 3500; right) has quite a buzz, especially when the glass wall is open. A tucked-away rooftop pool offers a quiet retreat.
Al Multaqa Street, T 403 3111,
www.livelaville.com

Vida Downtown

Eschewing the Arabesque style of the residential complex that surrounds it (the hotel was converted from an apartment block in 2013), Vida's designers opted for sophisticated simplicity, rendered in a palette of white and beige. The result is easy on the eye and the spirit; a respite from the city's maximalism, felt from the moment you step into the airy, draped lobby. It attracts 30- and 40-somethings from Europe and the Gulf states, with few children about, and there's a cool resort vibe around the courtyard pool, despite its diminutive size and the fact that only a wall separates it from Downtown's main drag. There are two great breakfast spots: 3in1, which offers a buffet, and La Serre (see p056). The location in one of Dubai's walkable areas is a plus, as is its proximity to The Dubai Mall (if that's your thing). *Mohammed bin Rashid Boulevard, T 428 6888, www.vida-hotels.com*

One&Only The Palm
The neo-Andalusian interior here is an essay in cappuccino marble, arabesque archways and glossy inlaid floors (lobby, pictured); the rooms, suites and villas are similarly chic. Secure a cabana by the enormous pool, and have tapas and cocktails on the pier, which affords a super panorama of the mainland skyline. *West Crescent, The Palm Jumeirah, T 440 1010, thepalm.oneandonlyresorts.com*

24 HOURS

SEE THE BEST OF THE CITY IN JUST ONE DAY

You may wish to tackle this itinerary differently if your timings are off, as rush-hour traffic (5pm to 7.30pm) is horrendous. We have plumped for a roughly chronological order, from old to new, even though most of it is, well, new. Begin in Deira, where Al Ahmadiya (opposite) reveals how Gulf architecture was before the glass and steel, and browse the souks for gold, frankincense and myrrh. Cross the Creek by water taxi to lose yourself in Bastakiya's maze of early 20th-century buildings. Break for lunch in DIFC at La Cantine du Faubourg (Emirates Towers, T 352 7105), which has a chic vibe and zingy mod-Med dishes, or at buzzy, funky Zaroob (Jumeirah Tower Building, T 327 6262), for the Levantine street food, or health café Inn the Park (T 056 565 5664), beside a brutalist classic (see p074).

Next it's time for an art fix in Alserkal Avenue, where the pick of the homegrown galleries is The Third Line (see p034), Isabelle van den Eynde (Unit 17, T 323 5052), Carbon 12 (Unit 37, T 340 6016) and Ayyam (see p065). The Jean-Paul Najar Foundation (Unit 45, T 258 7078) was designed by Mario Jossa, a colleague of Marcel Breuer, and OMA devised Alserkal Project Space (T 050 556 9797), on the piazza. Head back via the coast to the Etihad Museum (see p036) for a handle on Dubai's 'history'. By now, you'll deserve dinner with views. We'd book Jaan (see p038) or At.mosphere (Burj Khalifa, T 888 3828), the highest restaurant on earth (what else?). *For full addresses, see Resources.*

09.00 Al Ahmadiya

Until the early 1960s, Dubai was just a big village on the banks of the Creek, divided into three districts: Shindagha, Bastakiya and Deira, and it's a wonder they still exist given the rabid construction. The Al Ras enclave is one of the best locales to view how the city looked before it discovered oil. It's now a mishmash of eras and styles, decay and restoration, that is home to a few spartan but beautiful coral stone and gypsum merchant houses. Al Ahmadiya, Dubai's first school, was financed by a pearl trader in 1912. The two-storey building is set around a sandy courtyard and has thick walls, reed ceilings, decorative arches and plaques inscribed with Koranic verses. In places, shell pieces and animal fossils are embedded in the coral. It's now a museum. Closed Friday mornings and Sundays. *Al Ras, T 226 0286*

14.00 The Third Line

Early champions of Iranian and Arab art, Sunny Rahbar, Claudia Cellini and Omar Saif Ghobash set the bar high when they opened their gallery in 2005, with Monir Farmanfarmaian, Farhad Moshiri and Youssef Nabil on the books. The Third Line has lost none of its edge, giving numerous artists their first solo shows in the region, including Sahand Hesamiyan and Sophia Al Maria, and continues to nurture newer talent like Emirati photographer Farah Al Qasimi. In 2016 the gallery moved into a cavernous space in the Alserkal Avenue hub, designed by architect Amir Rahbar, Sunny's father. A monumental staircase zigzags to an upper level, and the venue encompasses two galleries and an audio-video room. Closed Fridays and Sundays. *Unit 78/80, Alserkal Avenue, T 341 1367, www.thethirdline.com*

16.30 Etihad Museum

This museum opened in 2016 on the site where the rulers of the seven Gulf states signed the treaty to form the UAE in 1971. The 1960s buildings have been restored, the then-shoreline has been recreated as a pool, in which stands a 123m flagpole, and Moriyama + Teshima's new building is a triumph. Its swooping roof was designed to resemble a turning page, but is more evocative of a falcon's head – an equally powerful symbol here. Inside, the sparse collection is a reminder of how young the country is, although the sheikhs' shades, watches and pistols have a certain quirky appeal. However, the space is lovely. Most of the action is underground, reached via an undulating pathway that evokes dunes, while the beige stone and nutmeg-hued wood reference the colours of the desert.
1 Jumeirah Street, T 515 5771

20.30 Jaan

On top of the Sofitel Downtown, Jaan has breathtaking vistas, but this is not its only calling card. Dubai has a wealth of Indian eateries but recently a more sophisticated style has emerged, pioneered by Indego (see p060), and now taken up a notch by Mumbai chef Farrokh Khambata. Dishes that read bizarrely on the menu – naan with camembert, burnt chilli and truffle, escargots à la bourguignon with Bengali lime – explode with flavour (order multiple small plates). Presentation is original too: cold-smoke chaat comes in a wood casket emitting clouds of liquid nitrogen. Interiors by Neterwala & Aibara feature splashes of crimson velvet, mustard-coloured leather and Missoni fabrics against a brown-and-black backdrop, with stylised Indian motifs.
The Penthouse, Sofitel Downtown,
T 457 3735, www.jaandubai.com

URBAN LIFE
CAFÉS, RESTAURANTS, BARS AND NIGHTCLUBS

Nightlife in Dubai is expat-oriented and because alcohol is served almost exclusively at (five-star) hotels, it revolves around them. Comedy venues feature acts from London, Dublin or Sydney and dance 'clubs' (such as they are) host DJs who were in Istanbul the night before and will be in Barcelona the next. It's all a bit, well, blah. To escape the 'great indoors' and still enjoy a drink, head to the toes-in-the-sand Jetty Lounge (One&Only Royal Mirage, Al Sufouh Road, T 399 9999). The artisanal coffee craze has spawned a lot of wannabes, but you will find the real thing at The Espresso Lab (opposite), The Sum of Us (see p057) and, where it all kicked off, at Raw (Warehouse 10, Street 4A/Street 7A, T 339 5474).

The city is packed with franchises by multi-starred chefs, but the more interesting dining options are set in the less-manicured 'hoods. If you're not fussed about alcohol (or interiors), Bu Qtair (Street 2B, Umm Suqeim Beach , T 055 705 2130) serves a cracking fish-of-the-day, and Samad Al Iraqi (Jumeirah Beach Road, T 342 7887) can't be beat for Iraqi treats like *masgoof*. Feast on cheap-as-chips Pakistani dishes at Ravi (Al Dhiyafa Road, T 331 5353), and explore Karama for no-frills Indian. Proper Emirati fare is hard to find, so if you fancy *dango*, you'll have to hit the tourist traps. Try Local House (51 Al Bastakiya, T 354 0705) or the dancing-camels-with-buffet blowout at Al Hadheerah (Bab Al Shams, T 809 6194). *For full addresses, see Resources.*

The Espresso Lab

Owner Ibrahim Al Mallouhi's appreciation for craft coffee was established as a child; his grandmother was a keen home-roaster. His approach here is that of a purist. The Espresso Lab only serves coffee, croissants and San Pellegrino to cleanse the palate. Staff are as enthused as the boss, who's often behind the counter, and will chat at length about origin – beans are sourced from micro-lots in far-flung places such as Burundi and Rwanda – and roasting times. It's set in a revamped villa on a residential street, lending the café an air of a secret shared among the Emirati and European regulars. Join them at the long, wooden communal table or on the linen-covered sofas dotted about the wide verandah.
The Hundred Wellness Centre, Street 53B, Jumeirah 1, T 050 421 1188, www.theespressolab.com

Coya

Normally, the hotter a restaurant is on opening in Dubai, the faster it goes cold. Not so here, as Coya is run by the same team that's kept Zuma (see p061) in fine form. It's a lot like the London original, with riotous decor (by Sagrada) melding faded colonial aristo with Andes market ethnic, and zingy Peruvian flavours. *Four Seasons at Jumeirah Beach, T 316 9600, www.coyarestaurant.com*

Stomping Grounds

Emiratis can often seem as scarce as snow leopards in the city (they make up about a tenth of Dubai's population), but not at this neighbourhood café. Since opening in 2016, it has been adopted as a de facto club by 20- and 30-something locals. The coffee is a big part of the draw – it roasts its own beans on the premises and offers all of the essential craft options, from cold brew to Chemex to Steampunk – as is the urban salvage decor, featuring polished concrete floors and industrial lighting. The menu is light and fresh (poached eggs on smashed avocado with toast, açai bowls), balanced by less guilt-free dishes (croque madame with quail eggs). It's open in the evenings but works better as a breakfast or lunch spot; there's also a small garden.
Villa 98, Street 12D, T 344 4451,
www.stompinggrounds.ae

Tom & Serg

The arrival of an Antipodean café culture is welcome here for many reasons – the relaxed service and fresh cuisine – but not least because it offers an alternative to the rivers-of-booze hotel brunches that have defined Dubai weekends for so long. Tom (a chef who hails from Melbourne) and Serg (a Madrid restaurateur) pour no alcohol at all, but what they do serve is done right. The two-storey property has been gutted and given a concrete-and-exposed-pipes interior, and is now touted as a 'warehouse'. It's quirky and fun, and the menu offers a hipster spin on comfort food, encapsulated by the salted caramel French toast, alongside some well-done classics, like eggs florentine. Refuel here if you're doing the Al Qouz gallery circuit. *Al Joud Center, 15a Street, T 056 474 6812, www.tomandserg.com*

The Artisan

With its dove-grey walls, velvet banquettes, parquet floors and rotating art displays, due to a partnership with Cuadro Gallery (T 425 0400) nearby, The Artisan feels very grown-up, as you might expect given its pedigree: it's an offshoot of the three-Michelin-starred Enoteca Pinchiorri in Florence. This is fine dining delivered in an entirely unpretentious style, based on the principle that first-class ingredients need minimal interference. Dishes such as pumpkin agnolotti and scallops served with cannellini bean purée are each worth multiple return visits, and the wine list is cleverly edited. Co-owner Firas Fawaz puts emphasis on building his smart clientele organically so, for now, you won't find it teeming with the see-and-be-seen crowd. *Burj Daman, Al Sa'ada Street, T 338 8133, www.theartisan.ae*

The Farm

On the dusty fringes of town, where only those optimistic enough to have made the International Academic City home would frequent, a vision in green has sprung up. Comprising more than 6km of canals and swathes of parkland, the development that is the Zaal family's Al Barari Villas rises from its stony surroundings. At its heart is The Farm, a café/restaurant ostensibly for residents, but actually open to anyone.

The healthy, fusion-influenced global menu includes the kinds of ingredients you'd find at a vegetarian love-fest. Meat-eaters are not forgotten, though, and some dishes can be tailored to requirements. Come for a morning yoga session, then lunch in one of the chic pavilions or terraces perched above the edges of a small, bird-filled lake. *Al Barari, Nad Al Sheba, T 392 5660, www.thefarmdubai.com*

Pierchic

Perched at the end of a pier, this dark, fortress-like place with its curious little wind towers looks somewhat gothic. The walkway can seem endless, but once you arrive, the laidback bar with a magnificent view of the sea and Burj Al Arab (see p015) make up for the exertion, especially after a premium Kir Royale. Pierchic is also a restaurant and, as befits its location, the menu is mostly seafood. The prices are steep, especially since the portions tend towards the *nouvelle*, although the high quality of the ingredients is evident in every bite. However, the real pleasures to be had here are of the liquid kind. So order a cocktail, settle down on a sofa lounger out on the deck and wait for one of Dubai's stunning sunsets.
*Jumeirah Al Qasr, Al Sufouh Road,
T 366 6750, www.jumeirah.com*

Marina Social

This Dubai outpost of Jason Atherton's restaurant group, opened in 2015, has the unmistakable Social vibe – a relaxed atmosphere, playful presentation, and not-quite-retro design – but it still feels completely its own. Scottish chef Tristin Farmer has developed the fresh menu specifically too, with twists on signature dishes; the Social Dog is made with duck and foie gras, and the burrata is stuffed inside a plump beef tomato. Local firm Draw Link Group has made great use of an unpromising, low-ceilinged envelope, creating a series of intimate spaces with wood-mesh panelling, and installing an impressive wine 'wall'. When the weather is right, though, the most coveted tables are on the terrace, with its Marina views. *InterContinental Hotel, Dubai Marina, T 446 6664, www.marinasocialdubai.com*

MusicHall

Imported from Beirut, where owner Michel Elefteriades has been making the best-clad booties shake for a decade, MusicHall has all the theatricality of its older sister. With red velvet, and plush seating and curtains, the venue is visually out of the 1890s, but even if the 'dinner and show' concept has been around since the Victorians, neither the meal nor the entertainment here are sedate. Known for his love of tango, reggae and Balkan gypsy madness, Elefteriades, the self-styled Emperor of Nowheristan (his unilaterally declared dominion has a flag), likes to mix things up – think classic Arab chanson set to *son cubano*. Although Dubai's clubbers haven't copied Lebanon's, who dance on the tables, rest assured that they know how to make some noise. *Jumeirah Zabeel Saray, The Palm Jumeirah, T 056 270 8670, www.themusichall.com*

Pantry Café

Publicly setting the bar high for itself, a Dubai proclivity, this café/deli in a rather unassuming building aims to be 'the place for breakfast, lunch, dinner and all meals in-between'. Presumption aside, it is a local gem and, although its look is more noughties than now, in terms of its ethics, support of artisan producers, pursuit of the organic and 'we are family' ambience, it is both old-timey and contemporary.

The flavours are decidedly 'international deli', and despite a few upmarket surprises, such as the lasagne with Wagyu beef, the feeling is more comfort than cosmopolitan. Most of the ingredients used to create the menu, as well as some choice ready-made preparations, are available to buy, so you can take a piece of the Pantry home.
Wasl Square, Al Hadeeqa Street,
T 388 3868, www.pantrycafe.me

La Serre

It used to be that if you fancied something French, your destination would have been La Petite Maison (T 439 0505). It is still a classic, but faces stiff competition from La Serre, a greenhouse-like box that wraps around the facade of the Vida hotel (see p028). Bishop Design's mirror-clad interior may say Cannes 1982, but Stéphane Cocu continues to produce a modern, seasonally observant set of sumptuous Med dishes and French classics, with an edge. The service feels almost invisible. You will not be 'persuaded' of the merits of your choice, but your waiter will have plenty of answers to your menu questions. It is less packed at night but still fun thanks to the open kitchen and buzzing bar. La Serre is a simple, sexy and succulent joy.
Mohammed bin Rashid Boulevard,
T 428 6969, www.laserre.ae

The Sum of Us

Tom Arnel and Sergio Lopez (see p045) have amped up two key elements of their first restaurant concept here: the coffee and the bread. Behind a glass wall on the ground floor is the roastery, and there's also an in-house bakery. While the setting in a new-build on corporate Sheikh Zayed Road is the polar opposite of Tom & Serg (gritty-but-hip Al Qouz), The Sum of Us has been given the signature industrial-style makeover, albeit softened with lots of leafy hanging plants. The upper level is rather soulless so hang out in the heart of the action. A short, snappy menu (all-day breakfast, lunch from noon, dinner after 5pm) is sprinkled with Middle Eastern and Aussie produce showcased in dishes like seared barramundi and crab claw fattoush. *Ground floor, Burj Al Salam, T 056 445 7526, www.thesumofusdubai.com*

The Rooftop Terrace
The view is less attractive now that The Palm occupies half the horizon, but this venue is as seductive as ever, known for its chillout soundtrack, cushion-strewn divans and serene ambience. It's all very *Arabian Nights*. Slip off your shoes, order a cocktail, and a plate or two of mezze, and forget that this damn world exists. *One&Only Royal Mirage, Al Sufouh Road, T 315 2414, www.oneandonlyresorts.com*

Indego by Vineet

You may eat in the company of Hindu gods and other tchotchkes, but the interior at Indego is sufficiently uncluttered to leave the focus on the food. Devised by Vineet Bhatia, whose now-shut Rasoi in London won a Michelin star, it still serves some of the best Indian food in Dubai a decade or so after opening in Grosvenor House (see p025). The menu is traditional with a few twists – ingredients include rose petals, truffle oil and morel mushrooms. Some dishes work better than others, but all deserve to be sampled. The pan-seared lamb chop biryani alone justifies a visit, and the paneer makhani, a cottage cheese in a rich fenugreek and tomato sauce, and 'gunpowder' prawns, which are prepared in coconut and spices, are also addictive. *Grosvenor House, Al Sufouh Road, T 317 6000, www.indegobyvineet.com*

Zuma

For its aesthetic impact alone, Zuma still impresses. The Japanese cuisine franchise occupies a double-height space in Dubai's financial district, the right location given the average price of a meal. Pull up a seat at the sushi counter, opt for a more formal setting in the lower-floor dining area, or hang out in the upstairs lounge, which has a striking bar (above) decked out with antique wood and backlit sake bottles. The signature dishes include crispy fried squid with a green-chilli-and-lime dressing, and miso-marinated black cod in hoba leaf. By day, Zuma draws a clientele that is often seen in the Square Mile, and if by night the jackets and ties disappear, conversations about barefoot pilgrims and bottom fishers reveal that this is still a trader crowd.
*Building 6, Gate Village, T 425 5660,
www.zumarestaurant.com*

INSIDERS' GUIDE

MASHHAD SHAH & ALICIA PAYNE, DIGITAL CREATIVES

Architect Mashhad Shah, from Pakistan, and advertising strategist Alicia Payne, an Australian, met here, and find the city's diversity consistently inspiring, very evident in their social media project Daakiya ('Postman' in Urdu). 'Its hidden corners are so at odds with the single-note, glitzy Dubai of popular imagination,' they say.

The pair like to spend Saturdays at Alserkal Avenue checking out the exhibitions, especially at Leila Heller (Unit 87, T 321 6942) and Gulf Photo Plus (Unit 36, T 380 8545), and refresh with a juice at Wild & The Moon (Unit 77, T 343 3392) or lunch at Hapi café (Unit 42, T 050 297 8384): 'It has great service and dishes bursting with flavour.' They take visitors to Bastakiya, to pop into galleries like XVA (see p024), and enjoy locally roasted coffee at cultural hub Creekside (off Ali bin Abi Taleb Street, T 359 9220).

In the evening, they might meet at Cocktail Kitchen (Cluster P, Jumeirah Lakes Towers, T 056 828 0727), for its 'retro tunes, sleek interiors and unique drinks'. Dinner is usually ethnic and simple, often in Satwa, where the pared-back decor and Filipino street food at Kalye Kusina (Al Satwa Road, T 352 1793) are 'a real find'. Another favourite is Goan institution Eric's (Block B2, Street 10B, T 396 5080), in Al Karama: 'Cheap, cheerful and always worth the trip.' For a nightcap, they highly recommend the breezy rooftop bar Iris (The Oberoi, Business Bay, T 056 951 1442): 'Good vibes.'
For full addresses, see Resources.

ART AND DESIGN
GALLERIES, STUDIOS AND PUBLIC SPACES

Unlike many of its Gulf neighbours, who have attempted to import culture from the top down by franchising global names, Dubai's laissez-faire approach has enabled an artistic community to grow organically. With little government meddling, a relatively tolerant attitude to self-expression (even if this has become a more delicate arena since the Arab Spring) and a business philosophy that fosters start-ups, there has been an explosion of galleries, and the Emirate has become a safe refuge for the region's creatives. This has afforded many the chance to gain international recognition, not least Saudi feminist Manal Al Dowayan, and Ramin and Rokni Haerizadeh, from Iran. Private initiatives, notably the Alserkal Avenue enclave (opposite), have added to the momentum, and in little more than a decade, the city has developed a vibrant scene. In March, Art Dubai and Design Days between them attract more than 130 galleries, and in November, Design Week has become a divergent platform.

In product design, a field once barely recognised, there is early evidence of a genuine local movement in which geometric motifs and other traditional Arabic references are reinterpreted with both subtlety and wit. Aljoud Lootah (see p068) and Khalid Shafar (see p069) lead the pack, while the work of those born overseas, from lighting designer and jeweller Ranim Orouk to ceramicist Michael Rice, bears the distinctive imprint of the milieu in which they live. *For full addresses, see Resources.*

Ayyam

Founded in Damascus in 2006 by Khaled and Hisham Samawi, Ayyam was one of the first galleries to set up in Alserkal Avenue in 2011, when it was all light industrial units and car-repair workshops. When the war made it impossible to remain in Syria, a second space opened in DIFC (T 439 2395). Ayyam brought the Syrian scene to the world stage, while providing a haven for those whose work challenged the regime.

Today, it also shows art from Iran and the Middle East. It has put on notable shows by Palestinians Samia Halaby and Khaled Jarrar; London-based Iraqi Athier Mousawi ('Machine Hearts', above); and the Syrian Tammam Azzam, whose work went viral in 2013 when he superimposed Klimt's *The Kiss* onto a bombsite in his home country. *Unit 11/12, Alserkal Avenue, T 323 6242, www.ayyamgallery.com*

eL Seed

Since his residency at Tashkeel (see p070), eL Seed has made Dubai his home. His mammoth calligraffiti-style murals adorn walls from Cairo to Rio, and his first commission here covers 30 sq m of The Green Planet facade in City Walk. Visit his Alserkal Avenue studio (pictured) to see more intimate works, and perhaps meet the artist in person.
Unit 75, Alserkal Avenue, T 346 1387

Aljoud Lootah

Trained in graphic design, Aljoud Lootah's background shines through in a penchant for geometry, seen in her origami-esque 'Oru' collection – a faceted chair, cabinet, mirror and light, in teak, felt and copper. Her Dubai roots are apparent too, in her reinterpretations of traditional culture and craftsmanship, and deconstructed Arabesque patterns. The carved Carrara marble ribs of her 'Unfolding Unity' stool (above) trace shadows cast by the eight-point star, while 'Misnad' is a wool carpet attached to a camel leather bench, inspired by Al Sadu weaving. 'What intrigues me about the patterns and motifs is that they reflect the environment – trees, piles of dates, sand dunes – in a very abstract way.' Her atelier is open by appointment. *106a Building 7, D3, T 050 670 4477, www.aljoudlootah.com*

Kasa

In the 'city that depends on others', Khalid Shafar's furniture and objects are actually designed by their maker, and the fact that he's Emirati makes him a role model, along with Aljoud Lootah (opposite). He is known for his public installations, such as 'Nomad', which travels (appropriately enough) but is often outside Building 1 in D3. Head to Shafar's polished concrete atelier, Kasa, to see his work. Pieces like the 'Illusion' stool, made from ash and Danish rope, and 'The Pattern' wallpaper and rug (above), a reinterpretation of 'The Seven Sands of the Emirates', using Pantone colours and the silhouette of Burj Khalifa, are a mix of the whimsical and the contemporary, and take their cues from the desert city's tribal beginnings and its rapid modernisation. *7 Street 22A, Community 612, Ras Al Khor Industrial 1, www.khalidshafar.com*

Tashkeel

Sheikha Latifa bint Mohammed bin Rashid is high up in the Culture & Arts Authority but back in 2008, as a working artist, she established not-for-profit studio space, incubator and gallery Tashkeel. Still going strong, it hosts regular exhibitions ('See Saw Seeds' by Ruba Al Araji, Tulip Hazbar and Yuki Tsukiyama, above), residencies, including the French-Tunisian artist eL Seed (see p066) in 2014, and workshops.

Set in a 1980s girls' school constructed in the typical style of an institutional building, this is the heart of the grassroots scene. Through its Tanween initiative, it supports emerging designers, among them Emiratis Zeinab Al Hashemi and Latifa Saeed, and Lebanese-American Zuleika Penniman. The alumni's work can be purchased online. *Nad Al Sheba 1, T 336 3313, www.tashkeel.org*

The Empty Quarter

Its claim to fame back in 2009 was that it was the first photography gallery in the region, but The Empty Quarter did not rest on its laurels, and has put on a succession of high-quality shows. Co-founded by Reem Al Faisal Al Saud, a talented photographer and member of the Saudi royal family, it has introduced Dubai to the work of global stars who have explored the Arab world, including Steve McCurry (above), as well as historic pieces, such as Christiaan Snouck Hurgronje's documentation of his travels in the 1880s. Nearby, also in Gate Village, the Farjam Foundation (T 323 0303) houses the private collection of the Iranian billionaire. Alongside ancient artefacts, contemporary Middle Eastern art features key figures like Ahmed Moustafa and Abdul Qader Al Raes. *Building 2, Gate Village, T 323 1210, www.theemptyquarter.com*

ARCHITOUR
A GUIDE TO DUBAI'S ICONIC BUILDINGS

Dubai's 21st-century skyline is the result of two things: the rush to build (the bigger the better) and the misconception that by calling every new structure 'iconic', it will become so. Unfortunately, most skyscrapers are no better than the anodyne glass-and-steel towers found in any global hub – despite a fancy topknot. It used to be that you could get away with such silliness. The majority of the Gulf was low-rise, so if you threw up a multi-storey, you claimed the cutting edge. Now that tall is the new normal, there's a dawning awareness that height alone does not confer validity; nor for that matter does a starchitect name. Marry this with the chastening 2008 crash, and it seems lessons have been learnt. The government is paying more attention to smaller-scale low-rise schemes such as City Walk (see p026), and repurposing disused areas, as in the D3 design district.

Then again, this is Dubai and there will always be fanfare – in 2016 ground was broken for a Santiago Calatrava monster higher than Burj Khalifa (opposite). Yet for every project that's announced, another is quietly shelved (or slowly sinks, as happened literally with The World Islands, although the official line is that all is still on track). If the Emirate does not continue to embrace quality over quantity, in a decade or so, when its neighbours come into their own, its star will wane. And if there were anything the city that hype built could not bear, it would be to surrender the limelight to its sisters. *For full addresses, see Resources.*

Burj Khalifa

From its wide base, this legendary tower, designed by SOM with Adrian Smith, spirals upwards, sections falling away, until its slim central core emerges in the top few hundred metres. Opened in January 2010, the world's tallest building soars 828m into Dubai's dusty sky. Its Y-shaped footprint is based on the geometry of a desert flower, but the impression of Gotham on Viagra is far too potent to miss. Islamic motifs are also alluded to, albeit in a largely symbolic manner, and many technical tricks include a double-glass skin that acts as a screen for light shows, and a lift that whooshes up to the 124th-floor observation deck (T 888 8124) in 60 seconds. The Armani Hotel (see p018) takes up 10 floors, and restaurant/bar At.mosphere (see p032) is on level 122. *1 Mohammed bin Rashid Boulevard, T 888 8888, www.burjkhalifa.ae*

Dubai Petroleum HQ
Legendary Palestinian architect Victor
Hanna Bisharat designed this zenith of
Arab brutalism. Built in 1978, it narrowly
averted demolition thanks to the 2008
crash. The concrete angles inwards like
a stepped inverted pyramid to combat
heat, light enters a central courtyard via
six-pointed stars, and huge gold screens
of Kufic script read: 'Praise be to God'.
Al Safa Street

The Index

Foster + Partners' 80-storey Index is an undeniably formidable presence. Austere and slab-like, it resembles a supersized monolith – a slender version of the Tyrell Corporation HQ in *Blade Runner* – and exudes a retro-futuristic chic. The office and residential tower (the functions are separated by a double-height 'sky lobby') opened in 2010, and is oriented east-west to minimise heat gain, while solar shades on the south elevation further lessen the sun's impact. As such, it is not only one of the city's most pleasing buildings (and few real pieces of design), it is environmentally laudable. A pedestrian boulevard, under construction in 2017, with an upper level seemingly inspired by NYC's High Line, will link it to the office complex at one end of DIFC and, later, The Dubai Mall at the other. *Al Sa'ada Street*

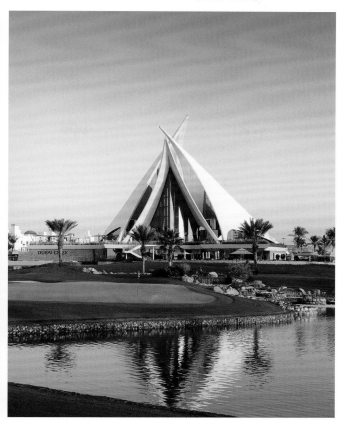

Dubai Creek Golf & Yacht Club

This golf course is not only conveniently located smack in the middle of town, but its clubhouse happens to be one of the most distinctive buildings in Dubai – look out for it as you cross the bridge on the way in from the airport. It was designed by UK firm Godwin Austen Johnson, known for championing a modern Arabian style at hotels such as the One&Only Royal Mirage. The sharply curving planes that intersect above the glass atrium are pure futurism, and pay homage to the sailing boats that formerly dominated the Creek. It has the essence of a Middle Eastern take on the Sydney Opera House, but most players probably don't notice, attracted instead by the par-71 championship course, and a nine-hole alternative floodlit until 10pm. *Baniyas Road, T 295 6000, www.dubaigolf.com*

Dubai Opera

Epitomising Dubai's don't-look-back-after-a-crisis ethos, a vast new 'cultural district' featuring a Zaha Hadid showpiece became, post-crash, a WS Atkins-designed opera house inserted into Downtown. Its scale is more humane than all the surrounding towers, and an outer skin of anti-reflective glass allows views in and out, by day and night, anchoring it to a plaza set by Burj Khalifa Lake. After dark, the timber-clad inner shell glows amber and assumes the shape of a boat, while in the auditorium, the stained-ash 'ribs' that form part of the acoustic engineering resemble the inside of a hull. A second key motif, mashrabiya, cleverly screens the 'stern' of the building and appears, in deconstructed form, on the interior walls. Such themes could easily have descended into kitsch, but instead it is a restrained, elegant addition to the city.
Mohammed bin Rashid Boulevard,
T 440 8888, www.dubaiopera.com

SHOPS
THE BEST RETAIL THERAPY AND WHAT TO BUY

Consumerism is a national sport here – well, when temperatures exceed 40°C, who'd want to kick a ball around? The sheer number of brands (tax-free but not cheap, since the 'Dubai discount' has more or less morphed into a 'Dubai premium') explains its appeal to visitors from China, Iran and Russia. But there really isn't much that a Londoner, Singaporean or Tokyoite couldn't find at home.

It isn't all bad. The souks are fun and atmospheric, if lacking in authentically Arabian goods. The Emirate is low on homegrown boutiques, but young native designers still pop up. In The Dubai Mall, check out the collections of Razan Alazzouni, Madiyah Al Sharqi and Noon by Noor at Symphony (T 330 8050), and the two in-house lines, Zayan the Label and By Sauce, at Sauce (see p086). For men, the Iranian Golkar brothers' Emperor 1688 (Souk Madinat Jumeirah, T 551 5484) offers a local take on luxe ready-to-wear.

What Dubai does well is custom-made goods. Head to bustling Al Satwa Road to pick up some fabric and take it to the nearby tailors, such as Dream Girl (T 349 5445) or, for the gents, Bespoke @ Deepas (T 344 5726). If you are tempted by jewellery, make a beeline for the Gold Souk (Old Baladiya Street) and the upscale Gold & Diamond Park (Sheikh Zayed Road, T 362 7777). And for gifts, you won't go wrong with a pretty box of dates, stuffed with candied orange peel, from Bateel (The Dubai Mall, T 339 9819).
For full addresses, see Resources.

Chi-Ka

Dubai is an unlikely place to find a kimono shop but its founders, Nemanja and Nina Valjarevic, have identified a close parallel in both form and cultural function between traditional Japanese dress and the abayas worn by Gulf women. The couple have art-world backgrounds and see the kimonos as canvases for creative expression; each is hand-painted or -embroidered. Chi-Ka also offers hybrid kimono-abayas, mainly black in the local tradition, but featuring swathes of floral designs between the knee and hem. All pieces are one-offs, with the most elaborate taking several months to produce (from AED6,500). The garments are hung like large-scale paintings in the double-height gallery, and the space hosts a roster of exhibitions and performances. *Unit 69, Alserkal Avenue, T 050 744 5911, www.chikaspace.com*

Comptoir 102

Tucked in an old villa, Comptoir 102 may not look like much from the outside, but through the door it's another story. Packed with character and well thought-out, it's a nifty mix of boutique and restaurant. There is a beautifully presented edit of fashion, furniture, interior objects, artwork and jewellery for the global nomad, much of it from France – core collections are by India Mahdavi and Astier de Villatte – and other pieces could be sourced from Japan, South Africa or Latin America. The menu shows the same attention to detail, and the food is fresh and local (not easy in the Emirates) and, if possible, organic, with vegan and gluten-free options too. The signature drink is black lemonade, made with maple syrup and activated charcoal.
102 Jumeirah Beach Road, T 385 4555, www.comptoir102.com

Boutique 1

On entering this multi-brand boutique, you might ponder why this sandy city is so obsessed with the all-white interior, but it makes a great backdrop for the array of clothes and lifestyle goods here. It's likely that the labels won't be new to you – JW Anderson, Isabel Marant, Acne, Common Projects – and many have standalone stores elsewhere in Dubai. However, the care with which the range is edited, and the excellent service, takes nearly all of the guesswork out of assembling a stylish wardrobe. The temptation to walk in and order one of everything (and as this is the Gulf, it's entirely possible this happens) is almost overwhelming. Also on sale within the two-floor space are home accessories and books, and there's another branch in the Mall of the Emirates (T 395 1200).
The Walk at Jumeirah Beach Residence,
T 425 7888, www.boutique1.com

Sauce Rocks

For a decade, Zayan Ghandour's fashion boutique, Sauce, sequestered in The Dubai Mall (T 339 9696) and Village Mall (T 344 7270), has sustained a cult following for its unorthodox labels. In 2015, Ghandour applied her eye for editing fresh talent to jewellery. The work of international makers, including some with Arab roots such as Suzanne Kalan and Noor Fares, is displayed beside collections from those based in the Middle East, like Beiruti Nada G, best known for her abstract rings made with precious stones and gold, and Ralph Masri, who crafts arabesque motifs into statement pieces. The interior riffs on a magpie's penchant for glittery objects; ceramic birds perch on the pendant lights and wooden battens represent the nest. *Galleria Mall, Al Wasl Road, T 344 0608, www.saucerocks.com*

Mirzam

For the proprietor of the UAE's first craft chocolatier, Kathy Johnston, a native New Zealander who moved to Dubai as a baby, there are no shortcuts. She sources raw beans directly from farmers, and the entire six-week process, from roasting to hand-wrapping, is done in Mirzam's production house-cum-shop. There are five single-origin bars, from Madagascar, Indonesia, India, Vietnam and Papua New Guinea, that are high in cocoa content, as well as themed lines infused with flavours like star anise, saffron, figs and dates. A Moroccan-inspired selection includes white chocolate with orange blossom and roasted almonds (above), from AED32, in packaging created by Qatari artist Aziza Iqbal. Tasting tours run at 3pm and 6pm, Tuesday to Saturday. *Unit 70, Alserkal Avenue, T 333 5888, www.mirzam.com*

ESCAPES

WHERE TO GO IF YOU WANT TO LEAVE TOWN

So much conspicuous consumption eventually wearies even the most ardent capitalist. When thoughts turn to escape, Dubai offers four options: the desert, the sea, another Emirate or a flight out. As for neighbouring cities, it is only in terms of development and amenities that the six other Emirates differ. That said, a trip to Abu Dhabi (opposite), Sharjah (see p098) or Ras Al Khaimah gives a sharper sense of regional context. Chilled-out alternatives include Isfahan (see p102); Muscat, where you should stay at elegant oasis The Chedi (North Ghubra 32, Way 3215, Street 46, T +968 2452 4401); and the wildlife-reserve island of Sir Bani Yas, which has a luxury retreat (Anantara Al Yamm Villa Resort, T 02 801 4200).

In winter, the desert has many draws. While it can be done in great comfort at Al Maha (Al Ain Road, T 832 9900), a tented resort in the midst of a vast game park on the city's doorstep, much of it is still rough and ready. You can visit hot springs (Ain Al Ghamour), ancient villages (Hatta), archaeological sites (Wadi Al Hayl) and go dune-bashing – Platinum Tours (www.platinum-heritage.com) organises trips in 1950s Land Rovers. A word of warning, however. Unless you're a connoisseur of kitsch, pass on packages combining an afternoon of adrenaline with visits to Bedouin 'encampments', henna tattoo sessions or belly dancing. For more edifying, design-led pursuits, hop to Saudi Arabia (see p092) and Qatar (see p093). *For full addresses, see Resources.*

Abu Dhabi

The UAE's capital floats on a sea of oil that the other Emirates can only envy. Smaller and less glitzy than Dubai, Abu Dhabi has retained traces of the modest fishing port it was when the black stuff was discovered in 1958. But not for long. Its bold ambitions are visible in edgy buildings such as the Yas Viceroy hotel (above; T 02 656 0000), which straddles the F1 racetrack, and Jean Nouvel's much-delayed Louvre, which is slated to open in 2017, on Saadiyat Island. On a more modest scale, the Manarat Al Saadiyat (T 02 657 5800) hosts top-notch exhibits, and Warehouse421 (Mina Zayed), converted from wharf buildings by BIG, is now a cultural hub. Even if you're not big on traditional Islamic architecture, Sheikh Zayed Grand Mosque is an exception. Only from inside can you appreciate its beautiful proportions and splendid stone marquetry.

Anantara Al Jabal Al Akhdar, Oman

Four hours by road from Dubai or a one-hour flight to Muscat followed by a two-hour drive, this is unarguably an escape. Architect Lotfi Sidirahal drew inspiration from ancient forts, and discrete sections of the resort circle the rim of the canyon, the axes between them established by stylised *falaj* (classic irrigation channels). The interiors feature accents of timber and antique brass, and Omani motifs have been distilled into a scheme of sage green, russet and beige textiles. The name means 'Green Mountain', and the 2,000m altitude provides a micro-climate ideal for growing pomegranates, walnuts and roses. There's a fine spa, and plenty to do, from yoga to abseiling. Or simply lounge in the infinity pool and wonder at the jaw-dropping view. *Nizwa 621, T +968 2521 8000, www.jabal-akhdar.anantara.com*

King Abdulaziz Center, Dhahran

This is one strictly for architecture buffs, worth a detour on the way to Bahrain. Commissioned by the state oil and gas company to mark its 75th anniversary in 2008, the snappily titled King Abdulaziz Center for World Culture (to give it the full name) is sited next to Saudi Arabia's first well, which began production in the 1930s. The design by Snøhetta is magnificent. A monolithic 90m-high organically shaped tower is surrounded by flatter-lying forms, reminiscent of a boulder field, and all are wrapped in stainless-steel tubing that acts as a sun screen. The heart of the building is three floors below ground – a metaphor for the source of the country's wealth deep in the oil fields. The sinuous lines carry on into the gardens, where pathways weave through indigenous desert vegetation.
www.kingabdulazizcenter.com

Museum of Islamic Art, Doha

Doha is hardly short of stunning modern architecture, it's just that nearly all of it is located within the campus of the Qatar Foundation and casual tours are, sadly, not possible. Thankfully, IM Pei's blockily beautiful Museum of Islamic Art, opened in 2008, single-handedly makes a trip to Qatar worthwhile. Rising 60m above the seaside corniche, this austere white exercise in geometry (overleaf), a dome that becomes an octagon that becomes squares that become triangles, is, without question, of today, but also references the past. Jean-Michel Wilmotte's minimalist interiors (above) are a showcase for one of the world's best collections of Islamic art, from calligraphy to ceramics. Daily flights from Dubai take about an hour.
Al Corniche, T +974 422 4446,
www.mia.org.qa

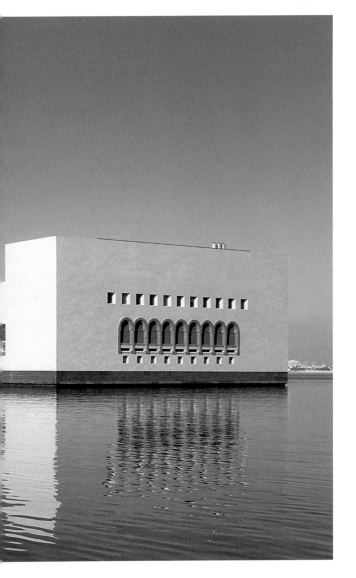

Liwa Oasis

Arrive in the UAE expecting *The English Patient*-style vistas and you may feel let down. The desert is vast, but rarely looks pristine or feels remote. Despite being a three-hour drive from Dubai, the oasis town of Liwa might not seem so either (perhaps it's the perfectly surfaced multi-lane highway), but drive a little further and you'll arrive on the fringes of Rub Al Khali (the Empty Quarter), a huge sea of sand stretching right across the Arabian peninsula. A diligently maintained road winds for 25km through dunes of myriad shades of beige, gold and brown to the rust-red Tal Mireb (Moreeb Dune), one of the world's highest, which rises 300m. On the other side of Liwa, head past the sleepy oasis villages and hard-scrabble camel farms to reach the Qasr Al Sarab Desert Resort (right; T 02 886 2088), where you'll find peace, pampering and night skies with zero light-pollution.

Sharjah

The Emirate of Sharjah doesn't look a bit like its gleaming neighbour. The high-rises aren't as high, the hotels haven't as many stars and the restaurants are a sober affair (nightclubs, alcohol, miniskirts and short sleeves are largely prohibited). In place of glossy malls, there are outdated shops and traditional bazaars. So why visit? Sharjah boasts many of the UAE's best museums, including those devoted to archaeology and Islamic civilisation, and hosts the Gulf's edgiest arts festival, the Sharjah Biennial, which takes over venues right across the city. Installations and exhibits are staged everywhere from the Sharjah Art Museum (T 06 568 8222) to the five complexes at Al Mureijah Square (Rayyane Tabet's *Cyprus*, above), and the courtyards of heritage buildings like 19th-century Bait Al Serkal (Thilo Frank's *Infinite Rock*, opposite).

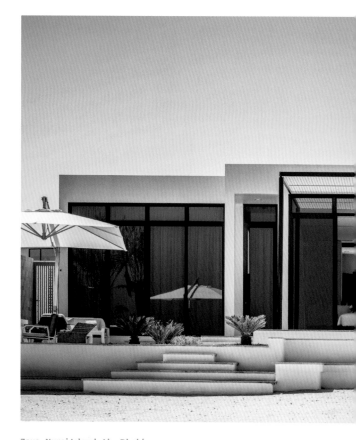

Zaya, Nurai Island, Abu Dhabi

One thing you're guaranteed not to find on Nurai is any trace of arabesque kitsch. Its clean lines and fresh white-on-white modernity would comfortably hold its own against Ibiza's finest. Another thing you won't find is camera-toting tourists; Nurai is reached via a 10-minute boat ride from the mainland, and values its privacy. The island's masterplan and its few residences were designed by New York-based Dror Benshetrit. Each of the 32 villas (nothing so basic as a room here; Beach Villa, above) has its own pool and vistas to the horizon. Dubai firm Etcetera Living has kept the interiors sleek, using shades of turquoise, white and beige. It's all so serene, you may never want to leave. If monophobia strikes, The Book Cellar (T 02 506 6274), our pick of the bar/restaurants, is the antidote.
T 02 506 6212, www.zayanuraiisland.com

DUBAI
A COLOUR-CODED GUIDE TO THE HOT 'HOODS

MARINA
This high-rise development is a cultural and leisure counterweight to Sheikh Zayed Road

AL QOUZ
Galleries and ateliers have moved in, adding a creative draw to a gritty industrial zone

DIFC
Within the glittering-glass business district are numerous fine-dining and nightlife venues

DEIRA
The tumbledown chaos of the real old town is a bustling reminder of Dubai's first boom

DOWNTOWN/D3
Home to the tallest building in the world, Downtown is fast becoming the city's nucleus

BUR DUBAI
There's a hotchpotch of heritage architecture and Indian restaurants in this 1960s 'burb

JUMEIRAH
Explore the boutiques, cafés and spas set back from this stretch of beachside playground

CREEK
A saltwater expanse and bird sanctuary is lined by golf courses and some rare green space

For a full description of each neighbourhood, see the Introduction.
Featured venues are colour-coded, according to the district in which they are located.

PHOTOGRAPHERS

Duncan Chard
Sheikh Rashid Tower, p011
W, pp022-023
Etihad Museum,
pp036-037
The Espresso Lab, p041
Coya, pp042-043
Stomping Grounds, p044
Tom & Serg, p045
The Artisan, p046, p047
The Sum of Us, p057
Mashhad Shah & Alicia
Payne, p063
eL Seed, pp066-067
Kasa, p069
Tashkeel, p070
The Empty Quarter, p071
Dubai Petroleum HQ,
pp074-075
Chi-Ka, p081
Comptoir 102, p082
Sauce Rocks, p086

Nagib Khazaka
Emirates Towers, p014
Al Ahmadiya, p033
Pierchic, p049
The Rooftop Terrace,
pp058-059
Zuma, p061

Raymond Meier
Imam Mosque, p102
Friday Mosque, p103

Mai Nordahn
XVA Art Hotel, p024
Indego by Vineet, p060
Dubai Creek Golf & Yacht
Club, p077

Walter Shintani
Cayan Tower, p010
MusicHall, p052, p053
The Pantry, pp054-055
La Serre, p056
Ayyam, p065
The Index, p076
Comptoir 102, p083
Boutique 1, pp084-085

Alamy
Deira Clock Tower,
pp012-013
Burj Al Arab, p015
Burj Khalifa, p073
Dubai Opera, pp078-079

Getty
Dubai city view,
inside front cover

**Courtesy of the Museum
of Islamic Art**
Museum of Islamic Art,
p093, pp094-095

WALLPAPER* CITY GUIDES

Executive Editor
Jeremy Case

Author
Sandra Lane

Deputy Editor
Belle Place

Photography Editor
Rebecca Moldenhauer

Junior Art Editor
Jade R Arroyo

Editorial Assistant
Charlie Monaghan

Contributor
Warren Singh-Bartlett

Interns
Nicole Alber
Electra Simon
Julia Young

Production Controller
Nick Seston

**Marketing & Bespoke
Projects Manager**
Nabil Butt

Wallpaper*® is a
registered trademark
of Time Inc (UK)

First published 2007
Fourth edition 2017

© Phaidon Press Limited

All prices and venue
information are correct
at time of going to press,
but are subject to change.

Original Design
Loran Stosskopf
Map Illustrator
Russell Bell

Contacts
wcg@phaidon.com
@wallpaperguides

More City Guides
www.phaidon.com/travel

PHAIDON

Phaidon Press Limited
Regent's Wharf
All Saints Street
London N1 9PA

Phaidon Press Inc
65 Bleecker Street
New York, NY 10012

Phaidon® is a registered
trademark of Phaidon
Press Limited

www.phaidon.com

A CIP Catalogue record for
this book is available from
the British Library.

Printed in China

ISBN 978 0 7148 7378 7

XVA Art Hotel 024
  Room rates:
  double, from AED600
  Near Al Fahidi roundabout
  Behind Arabian Tea House
  T 353 5383
  www.xvahotel.com
Yas Viceroy 089
  Room rates:
  double, from AED500
  Yas Marina
  Abu Dhabi
  T 02 656 0000
  www.viceroyhotelsandresorts.com
Zaya 100
  Room rates:
  Villa, from AED3,400
  Nurai Island
  Abu Dhabi
  T 02 506 6212
  www.zayanuraiisland.com

Al Maha 088
Room rates:
double, from AED2,800
Al Ain Road
Dubai Desert Conservation Reserve
T 832 9900
www.al-maha.com

One&Only The Palm 030
Room rates:
double, from AED1,000
West Crescent
The Palm Jumeirah
T 440 1010
www.oneandonlyresorts.com

Park Hyatt 017
Room rates:
double, from AED1,000;
Executive Suite, from AED3,400
Dubai Creek Golf & Yacht Club
T 602 1234
www.dubai.park.hyatt.com

Qasr Al Sarab Desert Resort 096
Room rates:
double, from AED1,200
1 Qasr Al Sarab Road
Abu Dhabi
T 02 886 2088
www.qasralsarab.anantara.com

Rove Downtown 016
Room rates:
double, from AED350
312 Al Sa'ada Street
T 561 9000
www.rovehotels.com

St Regis 016
Room rates:
double, from AED1,500
Al Habtoor City
Sheikh Zayed Road
T 435 5555
www.stregisdubai.com

Vida Downtown 028
Room rates:
double, from AED2,200
Mohammed bin Rashid Boulevard
T 428 6888
www.vida-hotels.com

La Ville 026
Room rates:
double, from AED1,300
Al Multaqa Street
T 403 3111
www.livelaville.com

W 022
Room rates:
double, from AED700;
Marvelous Room, from AED800
Al Habtoor City
Sheikh Zayed Road
T 436 6666
www.wdubaialhabtoorcity.com

Westin 016
Room rates:
double, from AED1,000
Al Habtoor City
Sheikh Zayed Road
T 437 3333
www.westindubaialhabtoorcity.com

HOTELS
ADDRESSES AND ROOM RATES

The Address Boulevard 016
  Room rates:
  double, from AED1,200
  Mohammed bin Rashid Boulevard
  T 423 8888
  www.theaddress.com

The Address Downtown 016
  Room rates:
  double, from AED850
  Mohammed bin Rashid Boulevard
  T 436 8888
  www.theaddress.com

Anatara Al Jabal Al Akhdar 090
  Room rates:
  double, from AED1,350
  Nizwa 621
  Oman
  T +968 2521 8000
  www.jabal-akhdar.anantara.com

Anantara Al Yamm Villa Resort 088
  Room rates:
  double, from AED1,550
  Sir Bani Yas
  Abu Dhabi
  T 02 801 4200
  www.al-yamm.anantara.com

Armani Hotel 018
  Room rates:
  double, from AED1,300;
  Armani Classic, from AED1,450
  Burj Khalifa
  1 Mohammed bin Rashid Boulevard
  T 888 3888
  www.armanihotels.com

The Chedi 088
  Room rates:
  double, from AED1,000
  North Ghubra 32
  Way 3215
  Street 46
  Muscat
  Oman
  T +968 2452 4401
  www.ghmhotels.com

Dukes 016
  Room rates:
  double, from AED1,000
  The Palm Jumeirah
  T 455 1111
  www.dukesdubai.com

Four Seasons DIFC 020
  Room rates:
  double, from AED750;
  Deluxe One-Bedroom Suite, from
  AED5,300
  Building 9
  Gate Village
  T 506 0000
  www.fourseasons.com/dubaidifc

Grosvenor House 025
  Room rates:
  double, from AED2,500
  Al Sufouh Road
  Dubai Marina
  T 399 8888
  www.grosvenorhouse-dubai.com

RESOURCES

CITY GUIDE DIRECTORY

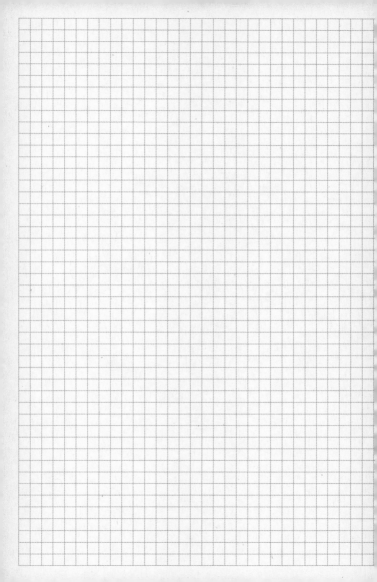

NOTES
SKETCHES AND MEMOS

Isfahan, Iran

A trip here requires planning (you'll need to organise a visa and reliable local guide), but Isfahan, Iran's equivalent of Athens or Rome, is immensely rewarding. A two-hour flight from Dubai, the beloved city of the Safavid emperors and twice the capital of Persia feels like a huge open-air museum. It's difficult to know where to start. What about Naghsh-e Jahan square (so large it is nicknamed Nesf-e Jahan or 'half of the world'), flanked by the frescoed Ali Qapu Palace and Sheikh Lotfollah Mosque, with its mosaicked dome? Or the dazzling Imam Mosque (opposite), or 11th-century Friday Mosque (above)? Or the restored Ali Gholi Agha Alley bathhouse, the Hasht Behesht palace, or the Armenian churches of Vank? Perhaps something older? If so, the ancient city of Persepolis and the tombs of Naqsh-e Rustam are a one-hour flight from here.